THE LOVE LETTERS
OF A PORTUGUESE NUN

Gabriel de Lavergne
Vicomte de Guilleragues

THE LOVE LETTERS
OF A PORTUGUESE NUN

With wood engravings by Simon Brett

Translated from the French by
Guido Waldman

THE HARVILL PRESS
LONDON

Originally published anonymously in 1669
with the title *Lettres Portugaises*

This translation first published in Great Britain in 1996
by The Harvill Press
84 Thornhill Road
London N1 1RD

3 5 7 9 8 6 4

English translation © The Harvill Press 1996
Wood engravings © The Harvill Press 1996

A CIP catalogue record for this book
is available from the British Library

ISBN 1 86046 034 8

Designed and typeset in Fournier
at The Libanus Press Ltd, Marlborough, Wiltshire

Printed and bound in Great Britain by Butler & Tanner Ltd,
at Selwood Printing, Burgess Hill

FOREWORD

By dint of persistent effort I have found the means to obtain a correct copy of the translation of the five Portuguese letters which were written to a gentleman of breeding who was on active service in Portugal. I have seen the letters praised or actively sought for by persons of some discernment in the matter of the tender sentiments, and thus I have considered I should do them a singular pleasure in having them printed. I do not know the name of the person to whom they were written, nor of the one who translated them into French, but it seemed to me that they would not be displeased if I made them public. It is scarcely possible that they would not have been published eventually with printing errors that would have disfigured them.

Only consider, my love,* how you have carried your lack of foresight to the point of exaggeration. You have been betrayed, poor thing, and you have betrayed me with false hopes. A passion on which you had founded so many plans to achieve pleasure brings you now nothing but a mortal despair; nothing can compare with it unless it is the cruelty of the absence that occasions it. This absence for which my distress, naïve as it is, can find no name sufficiently baleful, is it forever to deny me the possibility of looking into those eyes in which I saw so much love, eyes which introduced me to impulses of the spirit that filled me with rapture, that made up for everything, that in fact left me utterly fulfilled? Alas, my own eyes are deprived of the only light that inspirited them, all that is left to them are tears, and I have put them to no use beyond incessant weeping from the moment I learned that you were finally resolved upon a separation that I find so unendurable it will bring me to an early grave. And yet I feel in myself a sort of attachment to the pains of which you alone are

*Translator's note: This could refer to the object of the writer's affection, but is considered more likely to refer to the sentiments in her heart.

the cause: I dedicated my life to you from the moment I first saw you, and I feel a certain pleasure in making you a sacrifice of it. A thousand times a day I send my sighs in your direction, they look for you everywhere, and what is the reward for so much anxiety? They bring back to me nothing but an all too forthright premonition, the fruit of my ill fortune, and it is too cruel to permit me any self-deception but keeps saying to me: "Stop, wretched Mariane, stop eating your heart out in vain, stop searching for a lover you will never see again; he has crossed the sea to escape you; he is in France, in the midst of dissipations and does not spare one moment's thought for your sufferings. He dispenses you from all these transports which excite in him no feeling of gratitude." But no, I cannot bring myself to judge you so injuriously, and I have too much of an interest in exonerating you: I do not want to imagine that you have forgotten me. Why torture myself with baseless suspicions? Am I not miserable enough as it is? And why should I go out of my way to avoid calling to mind all the attentions whereby you manifested your love to me? I was so charmed by all those attentions, I should indeed be thankless if I did not love you with all the same enthusiasm excited in me by my passion, when I rejoiced in the testimony of your own. How can it be that the memories of such agreeable moments have become so cruel? Must it be that their only purpose now is to deny their own nature and play the tyrant in my heart? Indeed my heart was reduced to a sorry state by your last letter, which imbued it with a feeling as though it wanted to break loose in order to go and seek you out. I was so prostrated by the violence of these emotions, I spent three hours in a state of complete enervation. I refused to let myself return to a life I was to lose for you, since I cannot keep it for you. I saw the light once more, in spite of myself. I was pleased to imagine that I was dying of love, and besides, I was perfectly content to be no longer exposed to seeing my heart wrenched by the pain of your absence. After this experience I suffered a variety of indispositions, but can I ever be free of ills so long as I am not to see you? However, I endure them without complaint as it is from you that they come. Is that the reward you offer me for having loved you so tenderly? Well, never mind, I am resolved to adore you all my life and never to look on another person, and I assure you that you also will do well never to love another. Could you be satisfied with a passion less ardent than mine? You may possibly find greater beauty (though you did tell me once that I was rather beautiful) but you will never find so much love, and all the rest counts for nothing. Do not fill your letters with trivial things and do not write any more to tell me to remember you. I cannot forget you, nor do I forget that you gave me to hope that you would come and spend some time with me. Oh why do you not want to spend the whole of your life with me? If it were possible for me to abandon this wretched cloister I would not wait in Portugal for the fulfilment of your promises: I would go, heedless of all restraint, to look for you, to follow you, to love you anywhere in the world. I dare not flatter myself that such a thing could be, I do not wish to nurture a hope that would assuredly afford me some pleasure; I want to be receptive only to grief in the future. I will admit, though, that the occasion furnished me by my brother to write to you did surprise in me a certain impulse to joy and gave me a moment's reprieve from the despair in which I live. I do beg you to tell me why you took such pains to enchant me as you did when you well knew you were going to forsake me. And why were you so dogged in your effort to make me unhappy? Why did you not leave me in peace in my cloister? Had I wronged you in any way? But I beg your pardon: I impute nothing to you. I am in no condition to entertain thoughts of revenge, and it is only the harshness of my fate that I blame. It seems to me that in separating us it has done to us the worst we could have feared; it would be incapable of sundering our hearts; love, which is more powerful than he, has united them for the rest of our days. If you take any interest in my life, do write to me often. I certainly deserve your making some effort to advise me of the state of your affections and your fortune; above all come to see me. Farewell! I cannot be parted from this sheet of paper, it will drop into your hands; how I wished I might enjoy the same good fortune! Oh but how foolish of me, I can well see that such a thing is not possible. Farewell, I cannot go on. Farewell, love me always, and make me suffer even worse.

❊ II ❊

It seems to me that I do the gravest disservice to my heart's feelings in trying to acquaint you with them by setting them down in writing: how happy I should be if you could estimate them by the violence of your own! But I ought not to leave it to you, and I cannot prevent myself from saying to you, with a mildness which is far from reflecting my true feelings, that you should not mistreat me as you are doing by an indifference that drives me to despair, and that does you no credit. At least it is right that you should suffer my complaints about the sorrows I had fully predicted on seeing you resolved to forsake me; I well recognise that I deceived myself in imagining that you would act in better faith than is customary, for the excess of my love placed me, so it seemed, above all manner of suspicions and deserved a greater degree of fidelity than is normally to be found. All I have done for you ought to call forth in you a sense of fair dealing, but this has been overborne by your propensity to betray me. I should still be wretched enough even if you loved me for no other reason but my love for you; I should like to owe everything to your own inclination towards me. But I am so far removed from this state of affairs that

I have received not one single letter from you in six months. All this misery I attribute to the blindness with which I threw myself into an attachment for you: I should have foreseen that my pleasure would not outlast my love. What made me hope that you would spend your life in Portugal, that you would renounce your inheritance and your own country in order to devote yourself only to me? There can be no relief for my suffering, and the recollection of my pleasure fills me with despair. Alas, is my every hope to be in vain, am I never again to see you in my room displaying all the giddy passion you allowed me to witness! Oh how I deceived myself, knowing only too well that everything I felt in my head and in my heart was prompted in you yourself by nothing more than a few pleasures that were equally transient; in those moments of supreme happiness I should have called my reason to my aid in order to moderate the harmful excess of my rapture and warn me of all that I am now suffering. But I surrendered myself utterly to you, and was in no condition to call to mind that which might have poisoned my happiness and prevented me from deriving the fullest pleasure from the ardour of your passion. I took too much pleasure in the realisation that I was in your company to consider that one day you would be far away. I do recollect having occasionally said to you that you would make me miserable, but these terrors were dispersed soon enough, and I took pleasure in sacrificing them to you, and in abandoning myself to the spell of your protestations, your bad faith. The remedy to all my ills is clear enough to me, and I would not have waited to deliver myself from them were it not that I still loved you: but alas, what remedy is there! No, I would sooner suffer even worse than forget you. Does that depend on me, though? I cannot reproach myself of having desired for a single moment not to love you any more; you are more to be pitied than I am, and it is a far better thing to suffer all that I endure than to enjoy the languid pleasures you obtain from your mistresses in France. I am far from envying you your indifference, I pity you. I defy you to forget me entirely; I flatter myself that the condition in which I left you is such that your pleasures must be imperfect without me, and I am a happier person than you are, for I have more to keep myself occupied. I have recently been made portress in this convent; everyone who speaks to me thinks I am mad, and I have no idea what answer I make to them; the nuns must have been as mad as I am when they thought me capable of any office. Emmanuel and Francisco* are so carefree, how I envy them! Why am I not constantly with you as they are? I should have followed you, and I should assuredly have waited on you with the best of good will;

* Two little Portuguese valets. (Note in original editions)

there is nothing I ask of life but to see you. Do at least remember me. I am satisfied to rest in your memory, though I dare place no reliance on this; I did not limit my hopes to being remembered by you when I saw you every day; but you certainly have taught me to submit to your every wish. At all events I do not regret having adored you, I am only pleased that you seduced me; your intransigent and possibly eternal absence in no way diminishes the transports of my love. I want the whole world to know of it, I make no mystery of it, I am delighted to have done for you all that I have done in defiance of all conventions; I dedicate my honour and my religion solely to loving you passionately for the rest of my days, since I have begun to love you. I am not telling you all these things in order to oblige you to write to me. No, do not force yourself; I want nothing of you but that which comes from you spontaneously, and I reject every token of your love that you could find it in yourself to deny me. It would give me pleasure to pardon you, because you might derive pleasure from avoiding the trouble of writing to me, and I feel a deep-seated inclination to forgive you your every fault. This morning a French officer had the kindness to engage me for more than three hours in conversation about you; he told me that peace is made in France. If this is so, could you not come to visit me and take me to France? But I do not deserve such a thing; do exactly as you please, my love no longer depends on the way you use me; since you went away I have not enjoyed a moment's good health, and I take pleasure in nothing other than speaking your name a thousand times a day. Some of the nuns, who are aware of the deplorable condition into which you have thrown me, often speak of you to me; I leave my room as seldom as possible, the room you visited so many times; and I never stop gazing upon your portrait, which I value a thousand times more than my life. It affords me a little pleasure; but it affords me heart-ache as well, thinking that perhaps I shall never more set eyes on you; how can it be possible that perhaps I shall never more set eyes on you? Have you deserted me forever? I am in despair, your poor Mariane cannot go on, she is fainting as she ends this letter. Farewell, farewell, have pity on me.

◄◄✤ III ❧►►

What will become of me, and what do you want me to do? Everything I had been expecting is quite beyond my reach; my hope was that you would write to me from all the places where you stopped, and that they would be long letters; that you would foster my love with the hope of seeing you again, that I would derive some sort of peace from an utter confidence in your fidelity; and that in the meantime I would find my situation endurable, without any extremes of pain. I had even considered certain feeble proposals to try as hard as I could to cure myself, if only I could know for certain that you had entirely forgotten me. I seemed to be assured here of a wholly reliable assistance on so many counts were this to prove necessary: your absence, a certain sense of devotion, the fear of finally ruining what was left of my health with all those sleepless nights, all those anxieties, the small prospect of your ever returning, your coldness, the brusqueness of your final leavetaking, your departure on some rather ungratifying excuses, and any number of other reasons that are only too valid and yet to no purpose. In the end, having no one but myself to fight against, I was never able to put myself on guard against all my weaknesses nor be wary of all that I am now enduring. How pitiable my situation, being so alone in my unhappiness, being unable to share my pain with you. The thought of it is killing me; I am frightened to death at the thought that you never were more than moderately transported by our pleasures. Ah yes, now I am aware of the bad faith in those transports of yours: every time you claimed to be so happy at having me to yourself you were betraying me; your expressions of passion and ardour were occasioned by nothing but my own importunity; you took a perfectly calculated decision to set my heart afire, you looked on my passion merely as a victory, it never truly touched your heart. Are you not the unhappy one, are you not quite without feeling, to have profited from my transports in no other way but this? How was it possible that, heaping love on you as I did, I could not make you completely happy? I only regret in my love for you all those infinite pleasures that you have foregone; how could you not have wished to enjoy them? If only you had been able to recognise them you would assuredly have found a more exquisite satisfaction in them than in having deceived me, you would have experienced the far greater joy, the far greater emotional contentment that comes from loving with passion rather than from being the object of love. I do not know what I am, what I am doing, what I want:

I am torn by a thousand conflicting emotions. Such a deplorable condition is hard to imagine. I love you passionately and feel sufficient tenderness towards you not to dare, perhaps, to wish upon you the same emotional disturbance. I would kill myself or let myself die of grief without killing myself if I were assured that you know no peace, that your life is nothing but trouble and agitation, that you are constantly in tears, that you find everything hateful. I cannot cope with my own wretchedness, how should I ever be able to endure the pain that yours would procure me, for I would feel it a thousand times more keenly. And yet I cannot bring myself to wish that you gave me no further thought; and to be quite honest, I am furiously jealous of all that gives you happiness, of all that touches your heart and appeals to your taste in France. I do not know why I am writing to you, I see clearly enough that all I shall have from you is your pity, and I have absolutely no wish for your pity. I feel cross enough at myself when I consider everything I have sacrificed for you: I have forfeited my good name, exposed myself to the outrage of my parents, to the severity of the laws against nuns in this country, and to your ingratitude, which seems to me the worst misfortune of all. I do feel, however, that there is something false about my regrets, that I could wish with all my heart that I had incurred greater dangers for love of you, and that having risked my life and my honour gives me a macabre satisfaction; all that I hold most precious should be placed at your disposal, should it not? Should I not be only too delighted to have used it as I have? It even seems to me that I am not all that content with what I have endured, nor with the excess of my love, for all that I cannot, alas, flatter myself to the point of being content with you. I am alive, faithless that I am, and I am doing as much to preserve my life as to lose it: it makes me die of shame, as though my despair is confined to my letters. If I loved you as much as I have told you a thousand times, I would surely be long dead by now. I have deceived you, you are the one who should be complaining of me. Well, why are you not complaining? I saw you leave, I cannot hope ever to see you return, and yet here I am still breathing: I have betrayed you, I crave your pardon. But do not grant it me! Treat me harshly! Never accept that my feelings have been passionate enough! Be harder to please! Require me to die for love of you! I beg you to afford me this help, to enable me to surmount the weakness of my sex and put an end to all my hesitations with a genuine despair. A tragic end would no doubt force you to think often of me, my memory would be dear to you, and you may perhaps be touched by an extraordinary death: is that not of greater value than the condition to which you have reduced me? Farewell, would that I had never seen you! Oh but I am all too conscious of how false this feeling is, and I know, at the very moment of writing to you, that I should far prefer to love you unhappily than never to have set eyes on you; so I submit without a murmur to my evil fate, since you have not wished to improve it for me. Farewell, promise to regret me tenderly if I should die of sorrow, and at least promise that the violence of my passion may instil in you a sense of disgust and alienation from all else; this will be sufficient consolation, and if I have to abandon you forever I should want to leave you to no other woman. How cruel you would be to make my despair serve only to render you more attractive, to demonstrate that you have given away the greatest passion in the world. Once more, farewell. I write to you at too great a length, I am not sufficiently considerate, please forgive me, and I dare to hope that you will entertain some measure of indulgence for a poor, foolish woman who was not thus, as you know, before she loved you. Farewell! I feel that I am making mention too often of the intolerable state I am in; and yet I thank you from the bottom of my heart for the despair you cause me, and I loathe the tranquillity in which I lived before I met you. Farewell! My passion increases by the minute. Oh, to think of the things I have to tell you!

⤠✶ IV ✶⤟

Your Lieutenant has come to tell me that a storm has obliged you to put in to the Kingdom of Algarve: I fear that you will have suffered a great deal on the sea, and this dread has so preoccupied me that I have given no further thought to all my own troubles; do you really believe that your Lieutenant is more concerned than I am at what befalls you? Why is he better informed about it than me, and anyway why have you not written to me? I am truly unfortunate if you have found no opportunity to do so since you left, and even more so if you have in fact found one but still have not written; there are no limits to your thankless-ness and unjust treatment; but I should be heart-broken if these brought any harm down on your head and I should far sooner see them go unpunished than see myself avenged. If there are signs that ought to convince me of how little you love me, I resist them; I feel a far stronger inclination to surrender blindly to my passion than to heed the reasons you give me to complain of your neglect. Think what anxiety you would have spared me had you behaved from the first day I saw you in as offhand a manner as you evidently have of late! But who would not have been deceived, as I was, by such fervour, who would not have found it sincere? How hard it is to bring oneself to entertain suspicions for long as to the good faith of those one loves! It is clear enough to me that the smallest excuse suffices you, and you do not even need to take the trouble to make such excuses, my love for you serves you so faithfully that I simply refuse to find you guilty unless it be for the palpable pleasure of pleading your cause myself. You have enthralled me with your attentions, you have inflamed me with your ardour, you have charmed me with your amiability, you have reassured me with your promises, my unbridled inclination has seduced me, and what has resulted from these happy, these auspicious beginnings? Only tears, sighs, a grim death, all beyond my power to remedy. It is true that I have derived some quite unexpected pleasures from loving you, but these have been at the cost of an uncanny heart-ache, and the feelings you arouse in me are all so extreme. If I had stubbornly resisted your love, if I had given you occasion for dismay or jealousy in order to stoke up your passion, if you had seen something contrived or artificial in my behaviour, in a word, if I had tried to deploy my reason in order to check the natural inclination I felt towards you, of which you were quick to make me aware (for all that my efforts would assuredly have been to no purpose), you might punish me severely and take advantage of your power. But you already seemed to

me so lovable before you told me that you loved me;
you displayed to me a huge passion and I was delighted,
I abandoned myself to loving you without constraint.
You were not blinded as I was: why then have you
suffered me to arrive at the condition in which I now
am? What did you want to do with all this passion of
mine which could have been only an embarrassment for
you? You knew full well that you would not remain
in Portugal forever; why then did you come here to
choose me in order to make me so unhappy? You could
surely have found in this country some woman of
greater beauty, who would have procured you just as
many pleasures, since all you were looking for were the
grosser ones, and she would have loved you faithfully
for as long as she was seeing you; time would have
consoled such a woman for your absence, and you could
have left her without being heartless or treacherous.
Such conduct smacks far more of the tyrant who loves
to persecute than of a lover, whose only thought must
be to please. Why, oh why do you mete out such harsh
treatment to a heart that belongs to you? I see clearly that
you have been as easily persuaded against me as I was
readily persuaded in your favour. Without needing to
draw upon all of my love, and without being conscious
of doing anything out of the ordinary, I would have
resisted motives of far greater weight than those that
must have compelled you to abandon me; those would

have seemed to me quite trivial, and there simply are none that could have succeeded in tearing me away from you. But you wanted to take advantage of the pretexts that you found for returning to France: a ship was sailing; why did you not let it leave? Your family had written to you; are you unaware of all the persecution I have suffered at the hands of my own? Your honour obliged you to leave me; have I taken any care of mine? You were in duty bound to go and serve your king; if there is truth in all that is said of him, he has no need of your assistance and he would have held you excused. How happy I should have been if we had spent our lives together; but since a cruel absence had to part us, I feel I should be very satisfied that I have not been unfaithful, and I would not wish for anything in the world to have committed so black a deed. Look, you have known the depth of my heart and of my tenderness, and yet you could bring yourself to leave me forever and to expose me to the dread I must feel that you will no longer remember me unless it be to sacrifice me to a new love. I see well enough that I love you to the point of madness; and yet I do not begrudge in the slightest all the violence of my heart's passion; I am growing used to its persecution and I should not be able to survive without a pleasure I am discovering, and in which I rejoice, of loving you in the thick of a thousand woes. But I am ceaselessly harassed to my extreme discomfort by the

loathing and disgust I feel for absolutely everything;
I cannot abide my family, my friends, this convent; I
detest everything I am obliged to look upon, everything
I have to do out of necessity; I am so jealous of my
passion, I have the impression that all my actions, all
my duties are bound up with you. Indeed, I feel slightly
at fault if I do not devote every moment of my life to
you; oh but what would I do if my heart were not so
brimming with hate and love! Could I survive these
constant preoccupations of mine to live a quiet, languid
existence? I am not suited to such emptiness, such numb-
ness of feeling. Everyone has noticed the utter change
in my humour, my behaviour, my person; my mother
spoke of it sourly, but later with a certain kindness; I do
not know what reply I made to her, I suspect I made a
complete avowal. Even the austerest of the nuns show
pity for the state I am in, it makes them indeed a little
more considerate of me; everyone is touched by my
love, and you remain totally indifferent, never writing
to me except for cold letters full of empty phrases; you
leave half the page unfilled, and it is uncouth how plain
you make it that you are dying to get to the end of them.
Dona Brites kept on at me these last days to get me out of
my room; thinking to entertain me, she took me out to
walk on the balcony with the view over Mertola; I went
with her, and at once I was struck by a cruel memory that
had me in tears for the rest of the day; she brought

me back and I threw myself on my bed and brooded endlessly on the small likelihood I can see of ever being cured. Whatever is done to comfort me only makes me the more wretched, and even in the remedies I find special motives for affliction. I have often seen you pass this way with an air which I found charming, and I was on this balcony on the fatal day when I began to feel the first symptoms of my unhappy passion; it seemed to me that you wanted to endear me to you, even though you did not know me. I persuaded myself that you had picked me out from among all those in whose company I was. I imagined that when you stopped, you were pleased that I should have a better view of you and admire your address and your gracefulness* as you set spurs to your horse. I was surprised by a sense of apprehension as you were riding it past an awkward point; in a word, I took a surreptitious interest in your every action, I realized that you were not indifferent to me, and all that you were doing I attributed to myself. You know only too well what developed from these beginnings and, although I have nothing to be nice about, I ought not to set it down for fear of making you only the more guilty, if that be possible, than you are already, and incurring blame in my own eyes for so many useless attempts to oblige you to be faithful to me. That you will never be: am I to expect from my letters and my reproaches that

*The last three words are missing in the original editions.

which neither my love nor my dereliction have been able to effect on your thanklessness? I am too confident of my misfortune, your unjust treatment leaves me simply no room for doubt, and because you have deserted me I have everything to fear. It is not as if I were the only one to be captivated by you, other eyes will surely find you engaging. I believe I shall not be cross if the feelings awoken in others somehow justify my own, and I wish that all the women of France were attracted to you, that none fell in love with you, that none took your fancy: such an idea is absurd and impossible; still, I have sufficiently discovered that you are barely capable of a wholehearted passion and would need no help to forget me, you would not need to be constrained thereto by a new love. Perhaps I could wish that you did have some reasonable pretext. It is true that I should be all the unhappier, but you would be less to blame. I can well see that you will live in France without great pleasures, but in complete liberty. What is inhibiting you? Is it the fatigue of a long journey? Some notion of propriety? The fear of not responding to my transports? But have no fear: I shall rest content with seeing you from time to time and simply with knowing that we are in the same place. But perhaps I flatter myself, and you will be more responsive to the rigour and austerity of another woman than you have been to my favours; can it be possible that what will set you alight is ill-treatment?

But before you engage in a grand passion, stop and think, think upon the excess of my sufferings, the uncertainty of my plans, the turmoil of my feelings, the extravagance of my letters; think of my confidences, my desperation, my yearnings, my jealousy! Ah, you are going to bring unhappiness on yourself; I beg you to profit from the condition in which I am, and at least to derive some advantage from what I am suffering on your account! Some five or six months ago you made an unfortunate admission to me, confessing all too candidly that you had been in love with a lady of your own country. If it is she who prevents you from returning, let me know this without trying to shield me, so that I may not continue to languish. I am still buoyed up by some remnant of hope, and I should be quite relieved if I lost it for good (if it cannot lead to anything), and lost myself with it; send me her portrait with some of her letters, and write to tell me all that she says to you. I might find in them reasons for comfort, or for worse torment; I cannot remain any longer in my present state, and any change must be for the better. I should like also to have the portrait of your brother and your sister-in-law; all that has value for you is very dear to me and I am wholly devoted to everything that affects you: as to me, I have made no disposition of my own self. There are moments when it seems to me that I could be submissive enough to serve the lady you love; your ill-treatment of me, your scorn have so deflated me that sometimes I dare not even entertain the thought of jealousy for fear of vexing you, and consider myself utterly at fault for reproaching you. Often I am persuaded that I ought not to make a frenzied spectacle of my feelings, the way I am doing, as you disapprove of them. It is some time now that an officer has been waiting for your letter; I had made up my mind to write it in such a way that you would not be disgusted to receive it, but it is all too extravagant, I must bring it to a close. Alas, such a resolution is beyond my power; I imagine that I am talking to you as I write, and that makes you a little more present to me. The first one will not be so long, nor so importunate, you can open and read it on this assurance of mine; it is true that I am not to speak of a passion that you find disagreeable, and I shall not mention it again. In a few days it will be a year since I abandoned myself to you without reserve; your own passion seemed to me so burning, so sincere, and I would never have thought that my favours disgusted you to the point of forcing you to a five-hundred-league journey and the risk of shipwreck in order to escape from them: nobody owed me such treatment. You can recollect my modesty, my bashfulness and confusion, but you are quite unmindful of that which would compel you to love me despite yourself. The officer who is to bring you this letter has sent to me for the fourth time to say he wants to set out:

how importunate he is! No doubt he is forsaking some unfortunate woman in this country. Farewell, I find it harder to bring this letter to a close than you did to leave me perhaps forever. Farewell, I dare not address you with a thousand tender names, nor abandon myself unrestrainedly to a heart too full; I love you a thousand times more than my life, and a thousand times more than I think; how dear you are to me! And how cruel! You never write to me: I could not stop myself saying this to you once more; I shall start again, and the officer will leave. What does it matter if he does? I am writing more for myself than for you, I am only trying to obtain relief; anyway, the length of my letter will frighten you, you will not read a line of it. What have I done to be so wretched? And why have you poisoned my life? If only I had been born in another country! Farewell, forgive me! I dare not ask you again to love me; see to what my fate has reduced me! Farewell.

⊰⊱ V ⊰⊱

I write to you this last time, and hope to convey to you, in the revised terms and manner of this letter, that you have finally persuaded me that you no longer love me, and that therefore I am no longer to love you: I shall therefore take the first opportunity to return to you all I still possess of yours. Do not be anxious lest I write to you; I shall not even put your name on the package; I have left the arrangements all in the hands of Dona Brites, whom I had accustomed to confidences entirely remote from this one. I shall place greater reliance on her handiwork than I would on my own; she will take all the necessary precautions in order to be able to reassure me that you will have received the portrait and the bracelets you gave me. I want you to know, however, that for some days now I have felt ready to burn and tear up these tokens of your love, which I so treasured, but I have given you such a demonstration of weakness that you would never have believed me capable of going to such lengths. I mean therefore to exult in all the pain it has cost me to be parted from them, and afford you at least a little vexation. I confess, to my shame and to yours, that I have found myself more attached to these baubles than I should like to say, and

I felt the need once more to reflect fully in order to be able to part with each particular one, for all that I flattered myself that I felt no further attachment towards you; but one compasses whatever one wishes, on one pretext and another. I placed them resolutely in Dona Brites's hands, at what cost in tears! After any number of conflicting feelings and doubts of which you know nothing, and which of course I have no intention of imparting to you, I begged her never again to mention them to me, never to give them back to me, not even if I asked to see them one more time, and to send them back to you without telling me. I only became aware of the full strength of my love at the moment when I determined to make every effort to be cured of it, and I fear I should not have dared set hand to it had I been able to foresee such difficulties, such a wrench. I am sure I should have felt less of a horrible turmoil inside myself for loving you, thankless as you are, than in leaving you forever. What I felt was that I cared less for you than for my own passion, and I found it strangely painful to resist it after your offensive behaviour made me come to hate you.

The customary pride of my sex was of no help to me in hardening my resolve against you. I have, alas, endured your disdain, and I would have borne your hatred and all the jealousy occasioned in me by your attachment for another person; I should at least have had some passion to fight against. But it is your indifference that I cannot bear; your impertinent protestations of friendship and the ridiculous urbanity of your last letter showed me that you will have received all the letters I have written to you, but that they left your heart wholly unmoved, for all that you did read them. Thankless one, I am still foolish enough to be heartsick at the thought of not even being able to take comfort from the prospect that they never reached you, that they were not delivered to you. I detest your good faith: did I ever ask you to make a clean breast of things? You might have left my love intact! All you had to do was not to write. I was not looking for clarifications. Am I not wretched enough in having been unable to compel you to make some effort at deception, in being no longer in a position to find excuses for you? Rest assured, I am aware that you are unworthy of what I feel for you, I am acquainted with all your bad qualities. However (if all I have done for you may earn me some small consideration on your part for the favour I ask), I beg you not to write to me any more, and to help me forget you completely. Were you to give me even the slightest hint that reading this letter caused you some sorrow, I might believe you; and it could be that your avowal and your consent might irritate and anger me, and this could stir me up. So do not interfere with my behaviour, you would undoubtedly upset all my plans whichever way you handled the matter. I have no wish to know the outcome of this letter; do not disturb the state of mind I am adopting; it seems to me you can rest content with the harm you are already causing me, whatever plan you may have made to assure my unhappiness. Do not deliver me from my uncertainty; my hope is that with time I shall make something peaceable out of it. I promise not to hate you, I am too mistrustful of violent feelings to venture into hatred. I am sure that I may find here in this country a more faithful and a worthier lover. Alas, though, who could give me love? Would another's passion possess me? Did mine have any effect on you? Should I not feel that a heart that has been touched never forgets the one who introduced it to emotions hitherto unknown to it, but of which it was capable? That all its emotions remain attached to the idol it has created? That its first promptings, its first wounds can be neither cured nor effaced? That all the emotions brought to its aid, which attempt to satisfy it and requite it, do nothing more than bear empty promises of an inner sensitivity now beyond all recall? That all the pleasures it seeks, but does not wish to find, serve only to acquaint it with the fact that there is nothing it cherishes more than the memory of its sufferings? Why have you introduced me to the inadequacy, the mortification of an attachment that is not to last forever, and the pains attendant upon a passionate love, when it is not reciprocated? And why is it that a blind attachment and a cruel destiny generally insist on setting our hearts on those who are responsive to a different person?

Even if I could hope for some diversion out of a new affair, even if I were to find a person of good faith, I so deplore my own situation I should be very hesitant to place the last man on earth in the condition to which you have reduced me. And although I am not obliged to show you any consideration, I could not bring myself to wreak on you so cruel a vengeance, if it depended on me, by a change that I do not foresee. At this moment what I am trying to do is make excuses for you, and I realise that as a rule a nun is hardly a person to love. Still, it seems that if one were capable of finding reasons for* the choices one makes, one might form an attachment to them in preference to other women. Nothing prevents them from devoting unremitting thought to their passion, they are not disturbed by the thousand things that in the world occasion distraction and preoccupation. I imagine it is not all that agreeable to see those one loves endlessly preoccupied with a thousand trivial concerns, and one must be rather lacking in delicacy to endure, without being driven to despair, their constant talk of social gatherings, dressmakers' fittings, and outings. One is constantly exposed to fresh

*Variant in one of the original editions: capable of bringing reason to bear upon . . .

jealousies; they are required to show courtesy, complaisance, to make conversation: who can rest assured that they derive no pleasure from all these social occasions, that they always endure their husbands with an extreme distaste and an absence of good will? Those women ought to be wary of a lover who does not hold them to a rigorous account on that score, who accepts readily and happily whatever they tell him, and who remains easy in his mind and entirely trusting as he sees them submit to all these duties! But I do not propose to prove to you by good reasoning that you ought to love me; these are very shabby methods, and I have made use of far better ones with no greater success. I am too familiar with my destiny to try to overcome it; I shall be unhappy all my life: I was so, after all, when I was seeing you every day. I was frightened to death that you were being unfaithful to me, I wanted to see you the whole time, and that was not possible. I was anxious about the dangers you ran when you entered this convent. I was more dead than alive when you were on active service. I was in despair for not being more beautiful, more worthy of you, I grumbled at the mediocrity of my condition, I often thought that the feelings you seemed to have for me could be detrimental to you. I felt I did not love you enough, I feared for you as I thought of my parents' anger, in fact I was in as pitiable a condition as the one I suffer at present. Had you accorded me some token of your passion since you left Portugal, I would have made every effort to leave the country, I would have disguised myself to come and join you. Oh, but what would have become of me if you had taken no further interest in me after I arrived in France? What a convulsion! What bewilderment! What a peak of shame for my family, whom I dote upon now that I no longer love you. As you see, I am clear-sighted enough to realise that I might have been in an even more pitiable condition than the one I am in; and at least I am for once in my life addressing you in moderate terms. How my very moderation will please you, how gratified I shall make you! Well, I do not want to know, I have already asked you not to write to me any more, this I beg of you.

Have you never paused to reflect on the way you have treated me? Does it never occur to you that you have a greater obligation to me than to any person alive? I loved you to the point of madness; all I have received is disdain! Your conduct has not been that of a gentleman; you must have had an instinctive aversion for me as you did not lose your heart to me. I allowed myself to be seduced by some very mediocre qualities: whatever did you do that was supposed to captivate me? What sacrifice did you ever make for me? Did you not go in pursuit of a thousand other gratifications? Did you give up gaming and hunting? Were you not the first to report for active duty? Were you not the last to return from the army? At the front you took mad risks, even though I begged you to take good care of yourself for love of me; you never looked to find a way to settle in Portugal, where you were well regarded; one letter from your brother and away you went without a moment's hesitation; and I am not unaware that during the voyage you were in a thoroughly good mood. It must be confessed, I have to hate you like poison. Ah, but all my sorrows are of my own making:* first I accustomed you to a grand passion too naïvely, while it takes guile to excite love; some measure of address is needed to light upon the means to generate passion, and love on its own does not call forth love. You wanted me to love you, and in forming this objective, you would have taken no steps to achieve it; you would even have persuaded yourself to love me had this proved necessary, but you were aware that you could succeed in your enterprise without passion, and that you had no need of any. What bad faith! Do you think you could deceive me with impunity? Should some chance bring you back to this country, I promise you I shall turn you over to the vengeance of my parents. I have long lived in a state of unreserved idolisation that horrifies me, and I am persecuted with intolerable severity by my remorse. I am all too sensitive to the shame of the crimes you made me commit and,

*Original text which has given rise to conflicting interpretations respecting the authenticity of the letters.

alas, I no am longer possessed by the passion that
prevented me from appreciating their enormity. When
will my heart stop being torn? When shall I be delivered
from this cruel embarrassment? I believe, nonetheless,
that I do not wish you ill, and that I could bring myself to
consent to your being happy; and yet how could you be
happy if you have a heart? I want to write you a further
letter to show you that I shall perhaps be more at peace
in a while. What a pleasure it will be for me to be able
to tax you for the injustice you have done me once I am
no longer so sensitive to it, and when I make plain to
you how I despise you, to be able to say this in total
indifference to your betrayal, with all my pleasures and
pains forgotten, and in complete forgetfulness of you
except when I choose to call you to mind! I concede
that you have a considerable advantage over me, and that
you induced in me a passion which drove me to insanity;
but this should afford you scant self-satisfaction: I was
young, I was naïve, I had been shut up in this convent
since I was a child, I had seen only disagreeable people,
I had never heard the praises you were constantly
lavishing on me; it seemed to me that I owed to you the
graces and beauty you found in me and which you
brought to my notice. I heard good reports of you,
everyone spoke in your favour, you did all that was
necessary to give me love. But I have finally awoken
from this spell, you were of considerable help, and I

admit that I stood in urgent need of it. As I send back your letters I shall carefully keep the last two you have written to me, and I shall re-read them even more often than I read the first ones, so as not to relapse into my weakness. Oh but how dearly they have cost me, and how happy I should have been had you been willing to suffer me to love you forever! I realise well enough that I am still a little too much taken up with my reproaches and your infidelity, but bear in mind that I have promised myself* a more tranquil state and that I shall achieve it, or else that I shall take some extreme resolution against myself that you will learn of with no great regret. But I want nothing more from you. I am mad to keep saying the same things over again, I must leave you and spare you not another thought. In fact I think I shall not write to you again; do I have to give you an exact account of all the various things I am feeling?

* See previous note.

FINIS